THEY WORE

WHAT?!

The Weird History of Fashion and Beauty

Richard Platt

MINNETONKA, MINNESOTA

Contents

First published in the USA in 2007 by
Two-Can Publishing
11571 K-Tel Drive
Minnetonka, MN 55343
www.two-canpublishing.com

Editorial Director: Jill Anderson
Cover Design: Brad Norr Design

ISBN 978-1-58728-582-0 (HC)
ISBN 978-1-58728-584-4 (PB)

Library of Congress Cataloging-in-Publication Data on file

1 2 3 4 5 11 10 09 08 07

Printed in China

WARNING: *The practices in this book are for information only and should not be tried at home!*

Introduction

WHAT ARE YOU WEARING today? Are you a slave to fashion, buying hot new styles as soon as they hit the racks? Do you go your own way, mixing and matching individual pieces to create a look that's entirely original? Or do you shun fashion altogether, and just wear what's most comfortable?

However outrageous your style, you'll have trouble matching the most extreme fashions from distant times and places. Are you into piercings? How about wearing a plate the size of a saucer in your lip? Or if high heels are your thing, maybe you'd like to teeter around on the 30-inch (75-cm) monsters popular in 16th-century Venice, Italy?

In this book, you can read about these fashions and many more that you *won't* want to imitate. If some sound appealing, be wary of copying them. A waist you can wrap your hands around might turn a few heads, but you'd risk breaking some ribs to achieve it!

Would You Believe...? Would You Believe...?

When, where, who, which, what? When was there a fine for wearing fur? Whereabouts in the world did 600 women use makeup to kill their husbands? Who made the first bras? Which women had the tiniest waists? What fabric was worth more than gold? If you want to find out the answers, read on!

Fashionable Figures

S TARING DOWN from billboards or gazing out from glossy magazines, fashion models are sometimes hard to tell apart. Always tall, thin, and sculpted, they challenge us to lose weight so we can squeeze into ever smaller clothes. But it wasn't always like this. Ancient people had very different ideas of beauty.

Would You Believe...? Would You Believe...?

Fantastic fat
Not everyone agrees with the "thin is beautiful" idea. In southern Nigeria, tradition says rounder is better. Brides-to-be spent months in "fattening rooms," eating to gain weight. Movie stars in India were plump, too, until recently, when Western movies began to have more of an influence.

For Stone-Age folk, fat was fantastic! In a world where food was scarce (and there was a risk that tonight's dinner might bite back), a big body was proof of a person's strength

▲ **Stone-Age good looks**
Created about 6,000 years ago, this fist-sized pottery figure shows that Stone-Age artists admired shapely women who could provide many healthy babies. The "sleeping lady" came from the cave temple of Hal Saflieni, discovered in 1902

If you study paintings at an art gallery or pore over photos in a vintage magazine, you will see that the obsession with being thin is surprisingly new.

Artists like 16th-century painter Peter Paul Rubens show women as plump, happy, and attractive

Hourglass

In the 1950s, the perfect figure was an "8"—not a *size* eight, but a *figure* eight: a small waist between a fuller bottom and top. Only since the late 1900s has thin meant fashionable. Stick-like thinness is unhealthy, though. The truly trendy balance good looks with sensible eating.

Fuller film star ▶
American movie star Jayne Mansfield showed that curves were glamorous. She wowed movie audiences in the mid-1950s with her generous figure.

▲ Skinny chic
Fashion photos for designer Calvin Klein made English model Kate Mos famous in the 1990s. Her extreme thinness made it fashionable to loo like a waif (a starved young girl). Women have to endure permanen hunger and risk potentially dangerous diets to achieve this loo

Ancient
Attitudes

▼ **Egyptian beauty**
Painted some 3,370 years ago, this Egyptian woman is wearing a thin, almost transparent dress decorated with pleats (small neat folds). It covers half her chest, but many women wore nothing above the waist. In the hot climate, exposing some skin was acceptable.

S WELTERING IN the dusty desert heat of the Nile Valley, women in ancient Egypt had a hard time maintaining a fresh look. To keep their draped, see-through linen dresses beautifully crisp and clean, wealthy Egyptians changed clothes as often as four times a day.

• • • • • • • • • • • • • • • •

Rich and poor
Egyptian fashions changed slowly, but women and men showed off their wealth and style with collars, bangles, and belts of gold and precious stone. Poorer folk wore simpler jewelry made of colorful pottery beads.

▼ **Perfume cones**
In Egyptian paintings, men and women are often shown wearing "perfume cones" on their wigs, but nobody has ever found one. Artists may have drawn the shape to show that the wig was scented.

In ancient Greece and Rome, getting dressed meant winding yourself in yards of fabric. Pins and weights held them in place. Styles rarely changed, but fashionable women did not dare to wear last season's colors.

▼ Ancient Rome
The *stola* worn by Roman women was made from cotton, silk, or wool. It covered the whole body. In public, respectable women covered their heads, too. One Roman citizen, Sulpicius Gallus, even divorced his wife because she left the house with her head uncovered.

Most Egyptian men wore pleated skirts

◄ Ancient Greece
Ancient Greek men and women dressed in garments called *chitons*: long lengths of fabric draped over the shoulders and tied around the waist. This statue from the 4th century B.C. shows a woman wearing a cloak called a *himation* over her chiton.

Would You Believe...?

Costly clothing
Purple silk was the ultimate fashion fabric in ancient Rome. **Silk** was imported all the way from distant Asia and by itself was worth its weight in gold. But the purple dye made it even more costly! The dye was made from sea snails—10,000 of them colored just one garment.

One popular Roman fabric was made to look like clotted blood— it was black, but it sparkled in sunlight

Roman rule
In 218 B.C., Romans introduced sumptuary laws to control spending on luxuries. But they did not always work. In the 14th century, government officials tried to enforce them again.
The Romans in this crowd would have made the cut.

Forbidden Fashions

WOULD YOU pay a fine for wearing a silk hat, a gold ring, or a lace collar? If you'd lived in Europe 600 years ago, you might have had no choice! Special rules called **sumptuary** (spending) **laws** controlled who could wear fancy clothes and who had to dress in boring wool.

Sumptuary laws made sure that ordinary people did not look like noble men and women—those people whose families ruled the land. The laws also limited the amount of costly goods brought in from abroad, because buying them harmed the nation's trade.

Peasantly fashionable ▶
The poor people who grew crops to feed their rich, well-dressed masters had to wear woollen clothes, either undyed or in dull shades. English farm workers wore traditional clothes in these colors until the early 20th century.

Knights and merchants

King Edward III ruled in 1337 that nobody less important than a knight could wear fur (he later let merchants wear it—if they were five times richer than knights!). Sumptuary laws soon ended, but they set styles for working people's clothes until just a century ago.

In the 17th century, foreign lace was completely banned in France

▲ Jewels and gems
Bans on buttons seem strange now, but in the 14th century, buttons were often carved from precious stones. These Chinese buttons are made of jade, which only nobles were allowed to wear.

Coronation costumes ▶
The clothes worn by England's royal family on special occasions are rich in materials once controlled by sumptuary laws. The crowning dress (far right) is trimmed with ermine fur, which nobody below a lord could wear.

GARB BANS

FLORENCE, 1322
Silk and scarlet clothes can only be worn in the home.

ENGLAND, 1362
Yeomen and below cannot wear silk, silver, chains, jewels, or buttons.

PERUGIA, ITALY, 1366
Velvet, silk, and satin are banned.

FRANCE, 1583
Only princes can wear jewels and pearls on their clothes; gold and silver embroidery are banned.

CHINA, 1680s
Yellow clothing is off-limits for all except the emperor's friends and family.

9

Smooth
Operator

◄ **Roman tweezers**
Hair removal was a painful experience for rich Roman men and women. They had their slaves pluck out their armpit hairs using tools like the tweezers on the right in this grooming set.

BY SHAVING, scraping, waxing, or plucking, women since ancient times have tried to make their skin as smooth and hairless as polished marble. Most men shared their pain, cutting their chins daily with blades of stone or bronze.

In ancient China, dancers desperate for smooth skin removed hair with *rhusma*—a mixture of lime (a mineral that burns skin) and the poison **arsenic.** Later generations played it safer with tweezers or a rough stone called pumice.

▲ **Shaving stone**
Pumice stone, thrown out by erupting volcanoes, was one of the first razors. Its rough surface can be used to scrape off hair. English writer Samuel Pepys recorded in his diary for May 25th, 1662, that pumice shaved him "easily, speedily and cleanly."

Sugar solution ►
Sugaring is a hair-removal method first used in ancient Egypt and still popular today. A sticky solution of sugar, lemon juice, and water is pressed on to the skin, then stripped away, removing the hair at the root.

10

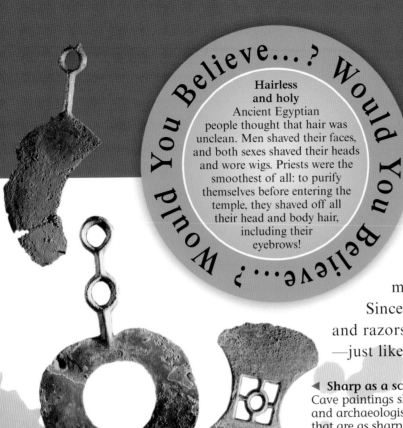

Hairless and holy
Ancient Egyptian people thought that hair was unclean. Men shaved their faces, and both sexes shaved their heads and wore wigs. Priests were the smoothest of all: to purify themselves before entering the temple, they shaved off all their head and body hair, including their eyebrows!

Medieval Christians once saw beards as ungodly

In 1915, advertisements first featured women with shaved armpits. The lie that hair was unhealthy made smooth skin fashionable. Since then, sales of waxes, creams, and razors have never stopped growing —just like the hair they briefly remove.

◄ **Sharp as a scalpel**
Cave paintings show Stone-Age men without beards, and archaeologists have found flint shaving blades that are as sharp as modern razors. When men learned how to make tools from metal, bronze razors like these replaced stone blades, but they were not as sharp.

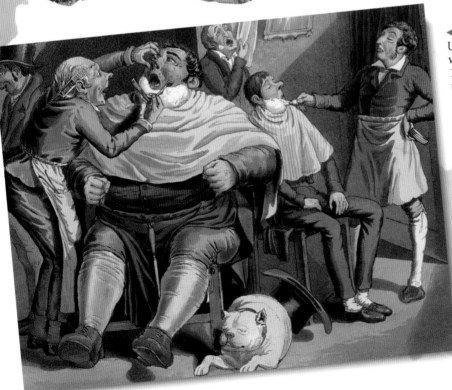

◄ **Sunday shave**
Until "safety razors" were invented in 1762, men shaved using sharp, straight blades. These were called "cut-throat razors" because, used carelessly, they could do exactly that. Many men preferred to trust the work of shaving to a barber rather than risk wounding themselves, as this humorous picture makes clear.

Fashion
Victims

CHECKING THE MIRROR, a fashion victim primps and pouts, adjusts a feather or two, then steps out—onto the battlefield! It isn't just **catwalk** queens who follow fashion. When soldiers from the past went to war, they literally dressed to kill!

Practical yet stylish

Until the 17th century, European soldiers wore whatever they liked, but this made it hard to tell friend from foe in the chaos of battle. **Uniforms** made a target of anyone in clothes that didn't match your own.

▲ French fashions
Medieval knights spent freely on fashion. Styles in **armor** changed quickly, and a new steel suit cost as much as a car does today. Parade armor was the most elaborate. Never intended for battle, it was decorated with brilliant colors, gold, and silver.

Samurai armor ▶
Japanese noblemen called samurai fought from the 12th to the 19th century in armor made of beautifully varnished metal and bamboo. They wore colored flags on their backs to identify themselves on the battlefield. Some wore elaborate helmets decorated with paper and leather nearly 3 feet (1 m) high or wide.

The red coats of British soldiers made them stand out clearly in the sights of their foe's rifles

17th-century European officers used their clothing to show off their wealth, adding rich **embroidery,** feathers, and gold. Armies became a glittering mass of color. This fashion parade ended in about 1890, when new uniforms in drab colors made soldiers harder to spot and shoot.

◀ **Emperor's finery**
Soldiers' uniforms were at their colorful best at the start of the 19th century. French emperor Napoleon Bonaparte, shown here, looked magnificent in gold buttons and trimmings. Even ordinary cavalry uniforms were made by the best Paris tailors and would cost the equivalent of $2,800 today.

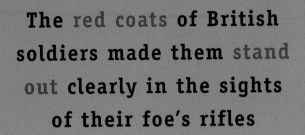

If You've Got It, Flaunt It

HOW LOW CAN YOU GO? When it comes to necklines, nobody went lower than the ancient Greeks. Their goddesses were pictured with tops that completely exposed their breasts. Ever since, women have tussled with "tut-tutters" in a battle over what is decent to reveal.

It's not just the bust that causes a stir. Even a glimpse of a woman's ankle can be shocking to some people. *What* you show is less important than *where* and *when* you show it. What's decent on the beach will raise eyebrows at the shopping mall!

● ● ● ● ● ● ● ● ● ● ● ● ●

◄ **Bare-breasted fashion**
In ancient times, Minoan women from the Mediterranean island of Crete may have worn costumes that showed off their shapely breasts. This picture is based on a pottery figure made 3,600 years ago for a religious ceremony. Minoan women were men's equals and even took part in sports such as boxing and bull-leaping.

14

The careful '50s ▶

Screen sweetheart Marilyn Monroe reveals almost all that was respectable on the beach in the 1950s. Yet just ten years after this picture was taken, American fashion designer Rudi Gernreich introduced the first topless swimsuits for women, which were briefly popular among the rich and famous.

Miniskirts got shorter in the 1960s as women's liberation moved forward. By 1967, they barely covered the bottom.

• • • • • • • • • • • • • • • • • • •

Keeping it covered ▶

For much of the 19th century, Western women's fashions covered the whole body, often concealing even the neck and ankles. Although exposed flesh was considered shocking, the same was not true of a woman's shape. Figure-hugging dresses showed off women's curves.

15

[Geismann hill
...]

Miss Beehive

BIG HAIR BEGAN IN ANCIENT ROME. Wealthy women employed an *ornatrix* to arrange their hair into high, wobbling piles. Women's hair did not reach the same heights again until the 18th century. Then topknots towered so high that they sometimes touched candles hung from the ceiling and caught fire!

▲ **High-rise hair**
The huge hair creations of the 18th century were constructed on high frames. Besides false hair, they sometimes included flowers, feathers, or even model ships. The sculptures were expected to last three weeks before they needed rebuilding.

● ● ● ● ● ● ● ● ● ● ● ● ● ●

Geisha hair ▶
Perfect hair was essential for Japan's geisha girls (traditional artist-entertainers). Starting in the 17th century, they combed their hair up into a style called *shimada*. The shiny black hair contrasted brilliantly with the geishas' white face makeup.

A geisha slept with
her neck up on a
wooden block to
protect her hair

The Beehive
This high-piled style was named after
dome-shaped beehives made from coiled
rope after aerosol hair spray that made it
possible was invented in 1948. Made from a
woman's own natural hair, hand and
heavy and could take hair to wash out.

Big hair was back in fashion in the 1950s, thanks to the invention of hair spray, which held tall styles in place. Men used greasy creams to sculpt **pompadours** that rolled over their foreheads like breaking waves. Big hair came back again in the 1980s. Styling gel and curling irons made multicolored **Mohawks** and poufy bangs easy to achieve.

Would You Believe...? Would You Believe...? Would You Believe...?

Horns of hair
Princesses of Tibet wore their hair sculpted into wide horns. Their maids wound their hair around light wooden sticks that stuck out 14 inches (40 cm) on either side of their head. The headdresses stayed in place all the time and made it impossible to roll over in bed.

A Hat for All Occasions

IF HATS DID NOTHING but keep off the sun and rain, most of them would look a lot alike: cheap materials, broad brim, little style. But hats do much more than this. They can tell the world who we are; how rich, fashionable, or important we are; and whether we are working or playing.

Hats pass on these messages because they are hard to miss when someone looks at us. And when a group of us wears the same hat, it says that we are all part of the same club or team.

The more beautiful the ladies, the higher were the steeples on their heads

▲ **High hats**
French and German women's hats reached a towering peak in the 15th century with a style called the "henin" or "steeple." A veil hung from the tip, sometimes falling all the way to the waist. When it became stylish for these giant hats to hide all the hair, women plucked or shaved their foreheads.

Poor beaver
In the 17th century, the best material for making men's hats was beaver fur. This was so scarce that a good beaver hat cost a laborer four month's wages and a maid one year's wages. Nations fought wars for the best beaver land, and trapping made beavers almost extinct in Europe.

▲ **Tricorne hat**
Men had worn hats with the brim cocked (turned up) in earlier times, but in the 18th century it became fashionable to cock three sides, creating a three-cornered, or "tricorne," hat. The hats were for carrying and posing only—they wouldn't stay put on their owners' huge wigs.

Hat fashions ▶
Bowler, top, and Panama hats were fashionable in the early 20th century. The bowler (left) was for everyday wear, the top hat (middle) for formal events like weddings, and the Panama (right) for vacations.

Ascot ▼
Each year on Ladies' Day at Britain's Ascot racecourse, women wear the most outrageous hats. The hats often make more of a buzz than the horse races.

Why wear a hat?

At first, hats were certainly made for protection—against the weather, accidents, or enemy blows. They do the same job today, but for many of us a hat also can be a bit of fun or the finishing touch for a fabulous outfit.

Monstrosities of 1827 ▼
Hats have often been an excuse for wild and weird decoration. This cartoon from 1827 makes fun of big hats by contrasting them with their owners' tightly squeezed waists.

Victorian women used long hat pins to defend themselves against pestering men

Wild and
Untamed

IN THE LONG GRASS OF ITS
Asian home, the tiger's stripes are a
perfect camouflage. They make this
elegant and powerful cat almost invisible.
On the back of a wealthy woman,
a tiger skin does the opposite,
making her appear to many
as cruel and uncaring.

Dressing in the fur, feathers,
and ivory of exotic animals
used to be the fashionable
way of showing off wealth
and status. Now it's a crime,
because hunting threatens
to wipe out some of the
world's most rare and
beautiful animals. A century
ago, there were probably
100,000 tigers. Fewer than
5,000 survive today.

▲ Pet trade
Furriers (people who make
clothes from fur) can
legally use cat and dog
skins in Europe, but not
in the U.S. Some
animal welfare
organizations
believe that
trade in pet fur
is cruel and are
campaigning
to stop it.

Fur coat ▶
Since humans first hunted, they
have valued fur for its warmth,
softness, and beauty. In 1954,
when this picture was taken,
there seemed nothing wrong
with wearing a coat made of
leopard skins. The growth of
the environmental ("green")
movement in the 1970s
changed many people's views.

In 2004, Tibetan customs officers **found the skins of** 31 tigers and 581 leopards **in a single truck**

Illegal trade

Since 1975, the Convention on International Trade in Endangered Species (CITES) has banned the sale of skins and other parts of endangered animals.

▼ Big cats

The beautiful coats of the big cats make them the most prized of all fur animals. They are at risk not only because of hunting, but also because the growth of cities, roads, and farms means they have fewer places to live.

Tiger (southern and eastern Asia)

Ocelot (South and Central America)

Jaguar (South and Central America)

◄ Prized plumes

The colorful feathers of birds of paradise once decorated hats. Hunting the birds stopped when it became clear that they were endangered. But today they are threatened once again, as loggers clear their forest homes in New Guinea.

Anti-fur protests

For some animal lovers, CITES does not go far enough. They believe raising animals on farms for their skin is also cruel. Their protests have stopped many fashion designers from using real fur.

▲ Faking it

Nobody has to wear real fur or skins to get the look they want. Manufacturers make realistic fake fur from artificial fibers. However, furriers argue that real fur from farmed animals is "greener." Unlike fake fur, real fur rots when thrown away and comes from a renewable source.

▼ **Boyish busts**

▼ **Boyish busts**
World War I (1914–1918) made women realize they were men's equals. They did the jobs of millions of men who had gone to Europe to fight. When the war was over, women showed off their new-found equality by dressing like men. The "flappers" of the 1920s cut their hair short and wore clothes that made them look flat-chested.

Bras and Bindings

BIG BUSTS OR SMALL? Fashion decides the shape, but it's a brassiere that provides it. Simple bras began in ancient Greece, with the *apodesme*—a rolled strip of cloth that lifted and supported the breasts. Roman women hid their breasts, binding them in a soft leather *mamilare*.

• • • • • • • • • • • • • • • • • • • •

The modern brassiere was introduced by the British fashion house Jaeger in 1904. It was marketed as a "bust girdle." It took on its modern name seven years later, when it went on sale in the U.S.

Would You Believe...?

Cantilevered bra
When actress Jane Russell was filming *The Outlaw*, the film's director, Howard Hughes, was unhappy with her costume. An avid pilot, he used aviation technology to design a special seamless bra with extra support. Unknown to Hughes, Russell never wore it because it was too uncomfortable.

Cones on top ▶

Madonna made her bra the center of attention on her 1990 "Blond Ambition" tour. Turning underwear into outerwear, she flaunted the garment as a fashion piece. Designed by Jean-Paul Gaultier, the cone-shaped cups copied and exaggerated the fashions of the 1950s. As planned, Madonna's outfit and act caused outrage, and the Pope called for people to boycott her show. It also inspired millions of imitations.

Fashion in bras alternates between the Greek and Roman shapes, either flaunting or hiding the breasts. Today, bras are the most complicated of all garments: some are made by hand from more than 20 pieces of fabric.

▼ Push-up revolution

Underwear that makes the cleavage look bigger is nothing new—it was popular back in the 18th century. But the modern version is a lot more comfortable. Stretch fabrics and padding provide support, and new microfiber fabrics give bras a super-soft feel.

Busts swell when business booms. Flat chests are fashionable during harder times.

Crinolines
and Bustles

▲ 18th-century *paniers* (French for "bread baskets") were worn to give dresses a wide look.

I N A DRESS THE SIZE of a small tent, how would you get through a door or sit on a chair? Wealthy women in the 16th century had to find ways to do these things because, beneath their skirts, they wore hooped frames called **farthingales** to spread out the fabric.

These women lived leisurely lives, so they could afford the inconvenience. But by 1850, the fashion had returned in the form of **crinolines,** worn by women of all classes.

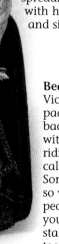

◄ **Farthingales**
The fashion for farthingales came from 15th-century Spain, where dressmakers used rope, woven grass, willow, or whalebone to stiffen skirts. By the early 1600s, fashionable women were lifting and spreading their skirts with hoops the shape and size of cart wheels.

Beastly bustles ▶
Victorian women padded out the backs of their skirts with huge and ridiculous devices called bustles. Some bustles were so wide and flat people joked that you could safely stand a tray of teacups on them.

▲ Crinolines
This humorous print shows just one of the problems that crinolines caused. Hoops of springy steel made going through doors and gates possible. But, as crinolines billowed to 6 feet (180 cm) across, women who tripped and fell could not even get up without help.

● ●

In factories, swirling crinolines caught in machines, and in fields, mud and rain clung to farm girls' impractical hooped skirts. The fashion didn't last long: within 20 years, the crinoline gave way to the **bustle,** which exaggerated the shape and size of womens' bottoms instead. To this day, bustles and crinolines are often worn to fill out fancy wedding dresses.

Special chairs
Crinolines changed the shape of the women who wore them, but they changed furniture, too. Sitting in a crinoline was tricky—all too often, the front sprang up. Special chairs with short legs and a sloping back left extra space for the yards of spreading fabric and solved the problem.

Farthingales were the most inconvenient and uncomfortable garments in history

Scaling down
Bustles changed from the 1860s, when they began to replace crinolines, until their disappearance around 1890.

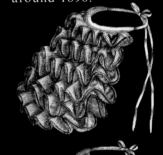

Construction ▲
Bustles started as "bum-rolls"—cushions tied above the hips to make a dress look fuller. Sprung steel hoops were introduced to make bustles lighter. Later, bustles got smaller, and their fullness came from layers of pleated fabric.

25

YOU CAN'T BREATHE. YOU CAN'T

walk. You can't sit down. A tightly laced **corset** may make your waist look tiny, but wearing one can be torture. Corsets are toughened, stiffened underwear. They are designed to squeeze the body into fashionable, often unnatural, shapes.

Invented 4,000 years ago in ancient Greece, corsets reached their most extreme at the end of the 1800s. In the U.S. and Europe, women of the times wanted a perfect wasp waist.

▲ Child-sized
Children's bones are soft and bendy, so adults believed that the younger they put their daughters in corsets, the less harm it would do. Underwear manufacturers usually recommended child-sized corsets, too— not for their slimming effect, but as a way of keeping a child's back straight.

◄ Menswear
Men wore corsets to slim their waists, as well as padding to emphasize other areas, such as their shoulders and thighs. In this 1819 cartoon, two servants helping to dress a stylish man are pulling on the laces that tighten his corset.

Not just for ladies
Beneath their starched shirts, some 19th-century men wore corsets to flatten their bulging stomachs. British prime minister Benjamin Disraeli wore one, and rivals of American president Martin van Buren claimed that he did, too.

Would You Believe...? Would You Believe...?

Fatal contraction
Corsets affected the health of millions, and occasionally even killed. In 1859, a French woman died three days after wearing a ballgown with a very narrow waist. An examination of her body showed that her corset had snapped three ribs, forcing them into her liver.

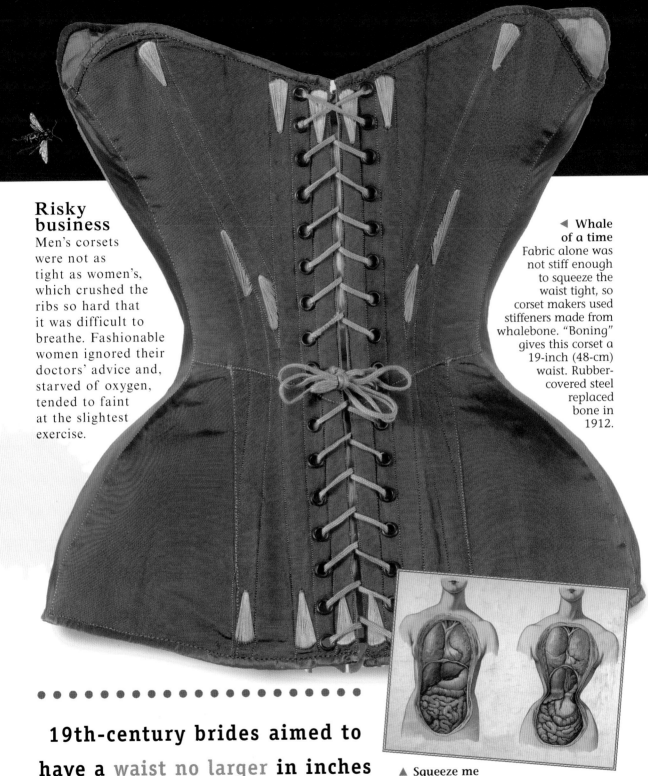

Risky business

Men's corsets were not as tight as women's, which crushed the ribs so hard that it was difficult to breathe. Fashionable women ignored their doctors' advice and, starved of oxygen, tended to faint at the slightest exercise.

◀ **Whale of a time**
Fabric alone was not stiff enough to squeeze the waist tight, so corset makers used stiffeners made from whalebone. "Boning" gives this corset a 19-inch (48-cm) waist. Rubber-covered steel replaced bone in 1912.

19th-century brides aimed to have a waist no larger in inches than their age—and most got married before they were 21

▲ Squeeze me
Tight corsets squeezed the body so much that the internal organs moved around and the liver almost split open. Besides shortness of breath, corsets also caused constipation and indigestion.

Squeezing and Shaping

▼ Cradleboards
Native Americans once carried their babies tied to **cradleboards**. It made a baby easier to carry and protected it from bumps. In the Northwest, some boards were designed to press gently on the child's forehead to give it a peaked shape. This was a sign of beauty.

YOU'RE NEVER TOO young to start thinking about fashion and beauty— that is, if you want tiny feet or a neck like a giraffe. Children's bones are so flexible that, by binding and pressing, parents have literally squeezed their children into the shapes they wanted.

The aim of this body-bending was to make children more beautiful. The families that did it lived mostly in times or places where ideas of beauty were very different from our own. What now seems cruel was normal to many in the 18th century.

Small is beautiful

Wealthy Chinese people began tightly bandaging the feet of their infant daughters more than 1,000 years ago. As the girls grew, the bindings broke their toes and deformed their feet, causing terrible pain. Binding a girl's feet showed how well off her family was: she was crippled, so she could neither walk nor work.

◄ Small slippers
Women with bound feet slipped them into unbelievably small shoes, some measuring just 4 inches (10 cm) from heel to toe. As walking was almost impossible, the shoes got very little wear and were made of fine materials. (Those shown here are silk.) Foot-binding in China ended in 1911 after the country's revolution gave women more rights and freedom.

Flat heads today
Parents no longer press or bind their children's heads on purpose, but one in eight babies develops a flattened skull naturally. The flattening, called plagiocephaly, occurs when a child sleeps every night with its head in the same position. Special exercises or headbands can correct the shape.

▼ **Long-necked women**
By binding their daughters' necks with brass coils, the Burmese Kayan people force down their ribs and shoulders, making their necks longer. If the coils are removed, they have to wear special collars until their withered neck muscles recover the strength to support their heads.

Foot-binding is now against the law, but another way of reshaping the body has not ended. In remote areas of South Africa and Burma, it is traditional for women to lengthen their necks. The number of rings is a sign of wealth. The women often wear matching bangles and leg-rings.

• • • • • • • • • • • • • • • •

A thousand years ago, Chinese men would not marry a woman if her feet had not been bound

29

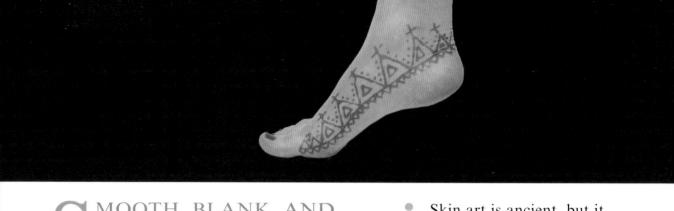

SMOOTH, BLANK, AND seamless, human skin is like an artist's canvas. No wonder some of us can't resist decorating it. Skin renews itself regularly, so marks on it soon fade. The only ways to make them permanent are to **tattoo** the skin by injecting dye under it, or to cut the skin to leaves scars.

Skin art is ancient, but it faded from use in Europe as Christianity spread. Some Christians believed that their holy book, the Bible, forbade marking the skin. The Jewish and Muslim faiths also put restrictions on tattooing.

Would You Believe...?

Tattoos and medicine

In many parts of the world, tattooing was a traditional way of protecting against disease. Samoan people believed that tattoos kept them from getting rheumatism. But tattoos do not stop disease, and may even spread germs if the needles used to inject the dye are not perfectly clean.

◀ **Maori faces**
Among the native Maori people of New Zealand, a man without tattoos on his face was once thought of as someone of no importance. The elaborate patterns were originally painfully applied with a sharp bone chisel. Dipping the chisel into soot made the swirling marks permanent.

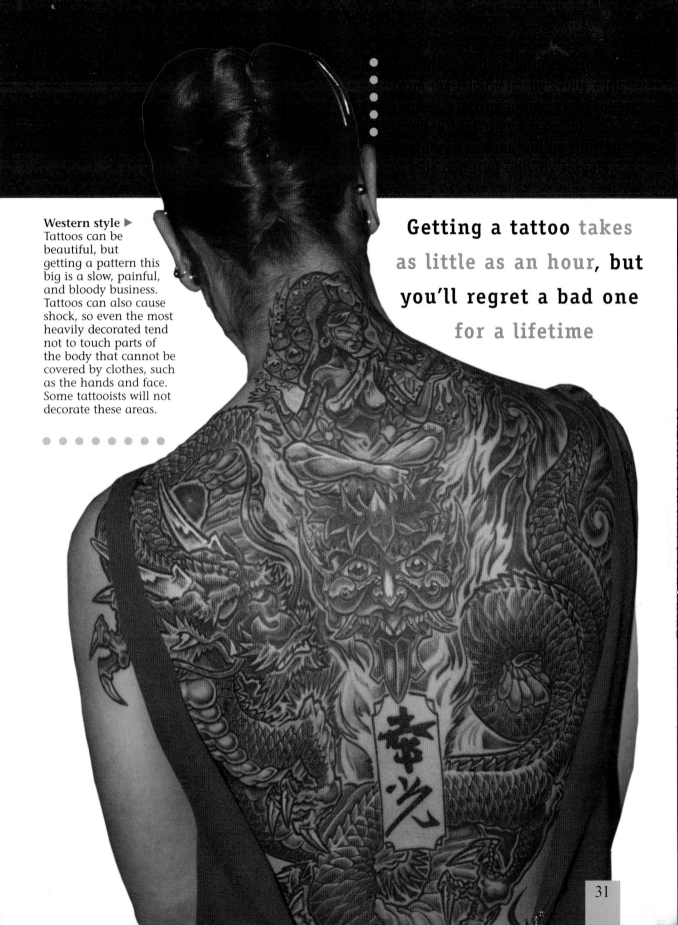

Western style ▶
Tattoos can be
beautiful, but
getting a pattern this
big is a slow, painful,
and bloody business.
Tattoos can also cause
shock, so even the most
heavily decorated tend
not to touch parts of
the body that cannot be
covered by clothes, such
as the hands and face.
Some tattooists will not
decorate these areas.

Getting a tattoo takes
as little as an hour, **but
you'll regret a bad one**
for a lifetime

My Feet Are Killing Me

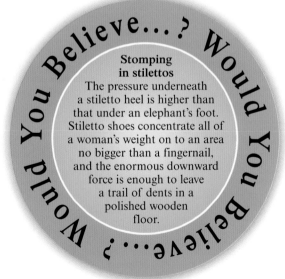

DANCING, WALKING, jogging, or just posing, a beautiful shoe shouts, "I've got style!" For centuries, the fashionable have spent big bucks on their feet, paying **cobblers** to make colorful and sometimes crazy footwear. At times, the styles have been so extreme that those who wore them couldn't walk.

Poulaines ▶
These shoes from the 15th century got their name, *poulaines,* from the French word for Poland—the country where they were first made. As fashions changed, the pointed toes grew longer and longer, until they were twice the length of the feet inside them.

◀ **Chopines**
Chopines were a type of shoe with a towering sole, fashionable during the 16th and 17th centuries. They were particularly popular in Italy. Women in the city of Venice wore chopines 2.5 feet (75 cm) high. This Venetian example is made of silk, wood, and leather.

These deliberately useless shoes showed that the owner was rich and never needed to walk more than a few steps. The shoes of poorer people were usually practical, comfortable, and waterproof, because they were always on their feet working.

Would You Believe...?

Stomping in stilettos
The pressure underneath a stiletto heel is higher than that under an elephant's foot. Stiletto shoes concentrate all of a woman's weight on to an area no bigger than a fingernail, and the enormous downward force is enough to leave a trail of dents in a polished wooden floor.

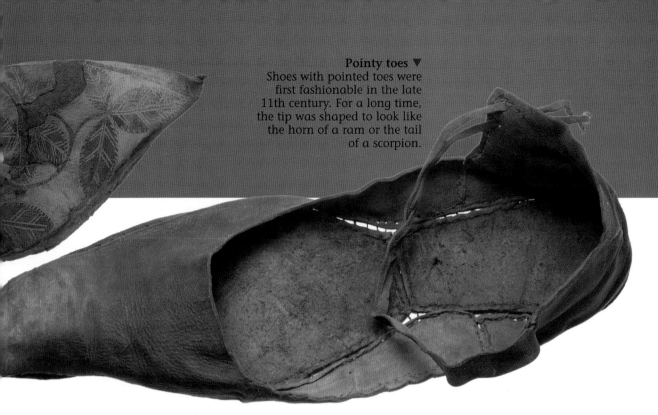

Pointy toes ▼
Shoes with pointed toes were
first fashionable in the late
11th century. For a long time,
the tip was shaped to look like
the horn of a ram or the tail
of a scorpion.

High heels were invented in Persia to keep feet out of the burning desert sand

Today, fashions in shoes change quickly, but surprisingly few styles are really new. Platform soles and pointy toes are centuries old. Only the **stiletto** has a short history—it was invented in Italy in the 1950s.

▲ Pattens
Shoe styles from the past were at their swankiest when the streets were muddiest. The way to keep expensive silk and velvet shoes clean was to slip them into **pattens**. These extra soles lifted your feet clear of the filth.

Deadly high heels ▲
Tall, narrow and dangerously pointed, stiletto heels were named after the thick-bladed daggers once used by Italian criminals. Though they make the leg look longer, they also make walking difficult and uncomfortable.

33

The Unkindest
Cut of All

THE FIRST PEOPLE to benefit from modern **plastic surgery** were not vain men and women, but injured soldiers. Blasted by shells and bombs in World War I (1914–1918), they had their shattered faces reconstructed by patient surgeons and dentists.

Would You Believe...? Would You Believe...?

Where'd by dose go?
To change the shape of a face, early cosmetic surgeons used some strange substances, including goose grease, white oak bark, and Vaseline. But the favorite was candle wax. Unfortunately, it softened in the sun, and patients found that their costly nose jobs melted on the beach.

Wartime experience gave surgeons new skills. American doctors were the first to use their skills to "improve" people's natural looks through **nose jobs** and **face-lifts.** Breast reduction began in the 1920s, but enlargement was not routine until the 1960s.

Changing faces ▲
Cosmetic surgeons today can completely change the appearance of the face—and even make a man look like a woman. British celebrity Pete Burns had a nose job and collagen (animal protein) injections to give himself a face (main picture) that he believed better fit his personality.

◀ **The first nose job**
Plastic surgery started in India some 2,000 years ago with the first nose jobs. Removal of the nose was a punishment for crimes such as stealing. Surgeons rebuilt it with a leaf-shaped patch of skin cut from the forehead. Flipped and lowered, it grew into a new nose. Wooden breathing tubes kept the nostrils open.

Obsession with youth and beauty has made cosmetic surgery a big business. But many of the operations carried out are unnecessary, and some of the clinics that perform minor treatments use untrained staff. Patients whose operations are botched need costly corrective treatment.

Not the knife
For a few, cosmetic surgery is essential. But for most of us, exercise, less sun and stress, and a healthier diet are safer, cheaper ways to improve our appearance.

One 15th-century German surgeon could "make a new nose if it has been lopped off and the dogs have eaten it"

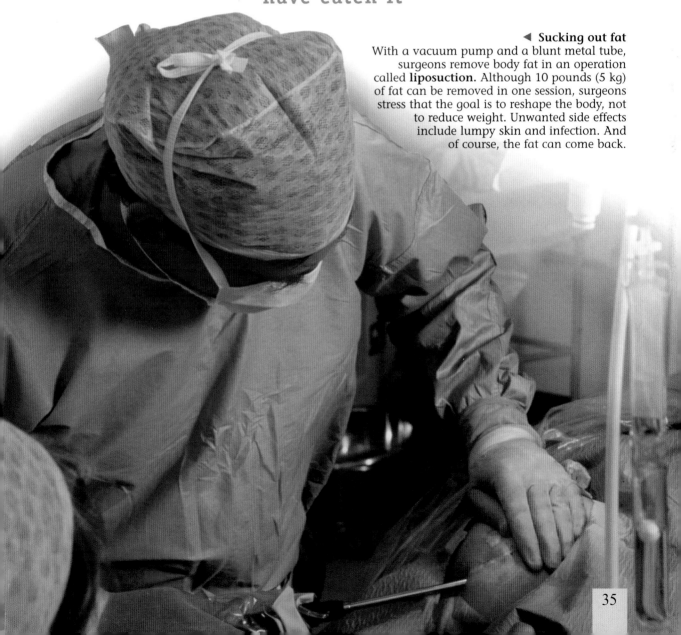

◄ **Sucking out fat**
With a vacuum pump and a blunt metal tube, surgeons remove body fat in an operation called **liposuction**. Although 10 pounds (5 kg) of fat can be removed in one session, surgeons stress that the goal is to reshape the body, not to reduce weight. Unwanted side effects include lumpy skin and infection. And of course, the fat can come back.

Why Stop at the Ear?

PROUDLY PIERCED punks may not know it, but their punctured lips, noses, ears, brows, and tongues celebrate a form of body decoration that is older than history. Nose rings are mentioned in the Bible, and some mummies from ancient Egypt have pierced ears.

For women in the U.S. and Europe, ear-piercing has always been popular. But few men wore earrings until the hippie era of the 1960s. **Body piercing** began in the U.S. some ten years later, and the trend spread.

● ● ● ● ● ● ● ● ● ● ● ● ● ● ● ●

◀ **Lip plates**
To make themselves more beautiful, Mursi women of southwest Ethiopia insert clay plates into cuts made in their lower lips. Gradually increasing the size of plate, they stretch the piercing to the diameter of a saucer. Many also stretch their earlobes with plugs in a similar way.

Radical or safe?

The risk of infection from a botched piercing is real, so don't try piercing even an earlobe at home. Avoid cheap jewelry and follow cleaning instructions carefully to avoid infection and speed up the healing of the hole.

King of the rings ▶

Cuban Luis Antonio Aguero claims to be the most pierced man in the world. Here, he is wearing 175 pieces of jewelry. Since this picture was taken, he has doubled the number of holes in his head.

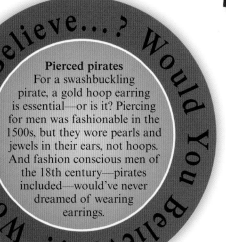

Would You Believe...?

Pierced pirates
For a swashbuckling pirate, a gold hoop earring is essential—or is it? Piercing for men was fashionable in the 1500s, but they wore pearls and jewels in their ears, not hoops. And fashion conscious men of the 18th century—pirates included—would've never dreamed of wearing earrings.

The Karankawa Indians of the Texas coast wore small pieces of cane through their pierced nipples

◀ Aztec lip plug

An Aztec nobleman would have worn this plug through his pierced lower lip in about 1500. At about 2.5 inches (6 cm) long, this lip plug is as big as some of the most extreme lip ornaments of today. The shaft is made from rock crystal, and the ends are gold.

All My
Own Teeth

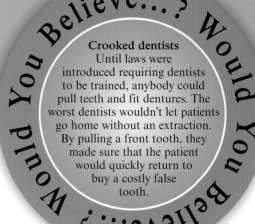
AT FASHIONABLE parties in the past there was little laughter. The jokes were funny enough, but guests kept their lips shut to hide their rotten teeth. Dental care improved in the 20th century, but only the rich could afford it. Just 40 years ago, four out of five older people had no teeth of their own.

The famous and fashionable hid their gaps with **dentures** (false teeth). Until about 1790, when **porcelain** dentures became popular, dentists carved them from bone or ivory, or took teeth from animals or from the dead.

Buying teeth
Wealthy people of the late 18th century found an alternative to dentures. Their dentists pulled out their bad teeth and pushed healthy teeth bought from poor children into the holes. These "live tooth transplants" lasted ten years.

First falsies ▶
In the 7th century B.C., the Etruscan people of Italy filled gaps using teeth that had been pulled. They attached them to gold bands that slipped over the remaining teeth. Nobody thought of a better way of holding teeth in place for another 2,500 years.

The fashion among Mayans in 9th-century Mexico was to decorate front teeth with jade and turquoise stones

▼ **Famous teeth**
In 16th-century England, false teeth were rare, so Queen Elizabeth I packed her mouth with cloth to fill out her sunken face. American president George Washington was not much luckier. His elk and human dentures were held together with powerful springs.

For those needing more than one or two teeth, wars provided a wonderful opportunity. When great battles ended, scavengers with pliers moved among the dead (and nearly dead), pulling teeth to sell. After the 1815 battle of Waterloo, London's rich wore "Waterloo teeth."

▲ **Washington kept his mouth shut to hide his dentures.**

Hippo teeth ▶
Ivory (the tusks of elephants and the teeth of hippopotamuses) supplied the raw materials for countless expensive sets of dentures. The plates and back teeth of this pair are carved from hippo ivory; the front teeth are human.

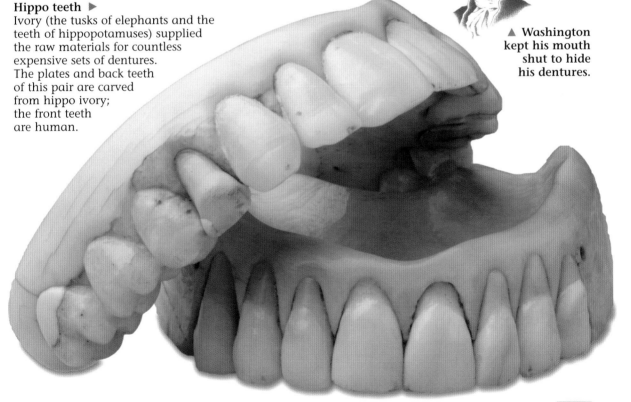

Makeup and Beauty

◀ **Greek rouge**
To redden their cheeks, ancient Greek women used the roots of alkanet, a plant of the forget-me-not family. Its red color contrasted with the white powder used elsewhere on their faces.

PAINTED WITH **rouge** and eyeliner, a beautiful face gazes confidently at us. Apart from her hat, this woman could be a modern fashion model, but she is from the 12th century B.C. As an Egyptian queen, her makeup would have been applied by a slave girl.

Over the following centuries, there has rarely been a time when women, and sometimes men, too, have not colored their faces for beauty—or to disguise their age.

◀ **Palace chic**
In this portrait sculpture, Queen Nefertiti's eyes are outlined with kohl (see page 42), and her eyebrows are painted. She is not, however, wearing the blue or green eyeshadow that was popular with Egyptian women.

▲ **Egyptian palette**
The ancient Egyptian name for makeup palettes like this one sounded the same as their word for "protect." Copper minerals used in some Egyptian eye makeup helped to prevent eye disease.

From Egyptian eyeliner to lipstick from Ur (now in Iraq), most makeup has ancient origins. Women relied on cosmetics made at home or by hairdressers and **pharmacists** until they were first mass-produced during the 20th century.

Egyptian workmen went on strike in 1158 B.C. because they ran out of eye makeup

◄ **Beautiful blokes**
In the late 17th century, European men were as painted as their wives. They powdered their faces, then applied rouge and lipstick. Velvet or silk hearts, stars, or moons, known as "beauty patches," completed the look.

Cult cosmetics ►
Makeup isn't always meant to make the wearer look younger or more beautiful. Shock-rocker Marilyn Manson uses radical cosmetics to emphasize his already dramatic features. The result is calculated to charm his young fans—and terrify their parents.

Poisonous Potions

MAKEUP TO DIE FOR sounds like a modern advertising slogan but, until laws controlled cosmetic safety, it was the truth. Many kinds of makeup contained poisons that, at best, blistered your skin. At worst, they killed you.

White face powders were among the most dangerous. The main ingredient of ceruse, the powder that every fashionable 14th-century lady wore, was poisonous lead. To redden their cheeks, wealthy men and women commonly used vermilion. This very expensive coloring contained **mercury,** a metal now known to be poisonous.

▲ **Deadly nightshade**
The Latin name for this plant is *belladonna,* or "beautiful lady." This name comes from its use: drops of the plant oil make the pupil of the eye bigger and more attractive. The plant's English name, *deadly nightshade,* reveals its other quality: if swallowed, it kills.

Would You Believe...?

Murderous makeup
17th-century Italian Tofana di Adamo sold a face-whitening makeup called *Aqua tofana* to other women. When 600 husbands died, Tofana was arrested. She confessed that the makeup contained deadly arsenic. Her customers used it to poison their husbands and inherit their money.

Kohl eyeliner ▶
This 3,300-year-old glass tube from Egypt once held kohl eyeliner, which was made from antimony. Small doses of this metal can cause headaches, dizziness, and depression. Larger doses are deadly.

16th-century women
used oil of vitriol
(sulfuric acid)
as a skin cleanser

▲ Pale and interesting
The white ceruse powder that England's Queen Elizabeth I used to paint her face scarred her skin. To hide the marks, she applied even thicker layers. By the time she died, Elizabeth's face looked like a white mask.

Poisons in clothes

Fashionable clothes and shoes have never been as toxic as makeup, but the people who make them have often suffered. Many people who made felt hats died of mercury poisoning, and the lives of leather workers in some parts of the world are still made shorter by the chemicals used in **tanning** (treating animal skins to convert them to leather).

Most cosmetics today are safe, but there are still dangerous levels of mercury in some skin-lightening products. And a few labels hide strange secrets: some expensive anti-aging creams are made from human **placentas** that were frozen and sold after women gave birth.

Mad as a hatter ▶
The Mad Hatter in Lewis Carroll's *Alice's Adventures in Wonderland* was driven "mad" (crazy) by his job. Until the 1940s, hatters used mercury to roughen the fibers of felt. It slowly poisoned them, causing twitching limbs, mental illness, and death.

In this Style
10/6

What's So Weird about That?

OUTRAGEOUS, DARING, extravagant, and sometimes even dangerous, fashion makes our world brighter and our lives livelier. Although we gasp at daring styles, a glance through this book shows that, in a different time or place, someone has almost always dressed in an even more amazing way.

Styles from different times and cultures make fashion more interesting and varied. You may not want to wear a towering wig, but the world would be a duller place if nobody ever had.

Would You Believe...? Would You Believe...? Would You Believe...?

Selling dreams
Most top fashion models are a size 8 or smaller, but the average women's dress size in the U.S. is a 14. No wonder it's so hard to find new clothes that fit you! The fashion industry may be selling a glamorous dream, but it is so far from reality that buying clothes can be miserable.

◀ **The catwalk**
Catwalk models show off styles that only the very wealthy can buy. Soon after a show, mainstream clothing maufacturers copy the styles to sell at lower prices. This way, a few top designers control the styles we all wear.

Fashion slaves
Fashion may seem like fun, but as you've seen, it can be ridiculous and harmful, too. Looking just the same as everyone else may be reassuring, but it is also expensive and wasteful. Why should this summer's colors, fabrics, and styles be different from last summer's?

Don't be afraid to escape from the herd. Be yourself, and wear something completely different!

Find Out More

You can find out lots more about the strange and surprising history of fashion and beauty from these books and websites.

Books

Cobb, Vicki. *Sneakers.* Minneapolis: Milbrook Press, 2006.

Galford, Ellen. *Festivals.* Broomall, Penn.: Mason Crest, 2003.

Gay, Kathlyn and Christine Whittington. *Body Marks: Tattooing, Piercing, and Scarification.* Brookfield, Conn.: Millbrook Press, 2002.

Kyi, Tanya Lloyd. *The Blue Jean Book: The Story Behind the Seams.* Toronto: Annick Press, 2005.

Lomas, Clare. *The 80s & 90s: Power Dressing to Sportswear.* Milwaukee, Wis.: Gareth Stevens, 2000.

Reynolds, Helen. *A Fashionable History of Jewelry & Accessories.* Chicago: Raintree, 2003.

Sills, Leslie. *From Rags to Riches: A History of Girls' Clothing in America.* New York: Holiday House, 2005.

Weaver, Janice. *From Head to Toe: Bound Feet, Bathing Suits, and Other Bizarre and Beautiful Things.* Toronto: Tundra Books, 2003.

Whitty, Helen. *Underwear.* Philadelphia, Penn.: Chelsea House, 2001.

Websites

Costume drama game
http://www.museumofcostume.co.uk/
    htmlContent/game.htm
Test your knowledge of fashion from four eras.

Design a textile
http://www.vam.ac.uk/vastatic/microsites/
    british_galleries/designa/textile/textile.html
Mix colors and patterns to design your own fabric sample.

Clothing in American History
http://americanhistory.si.edu/collections/
    subject_detail.cfm?key=32&colkey=8
View an online gallery of important and unusual fashion artifacts from U.S. history.

Kimonos
http://web-japan.org/kidsweb/virtual/kimono/top.html
Find out about traditional Japanese costume, and design your own kimono.

Corsets
http://www.vam.ac.uk/collections/fashion/
    corset/index.html
Discover the history of corsets and crinolines with this virtual exhibit of the Victoria & Albert Museum.

Henna tattoos
http://www.mehendiworld.com
The story of *mehendi* (henna tattoos), with practical instructions and designs to copy.

All about shoes
http://www.allaboutshoes.ca/en
Learn about high heels and more on this website.

History of sneakers
http://www.sneakerhead.com/sneaker-history-p1.html
All you need to know about athletic shoes.

Glossary

armor protective clothing worn in battle to prevent injuries.

arsenic a poisonous, metal-like chemical. One-twentieth of a teaspoonful would kill an adult.

body piercing using a needle to create holes in lips, eyebrows, or other body parts where jewelry can be inserted

bustle an undergarment for women that lifts the back of a dress away from the body

catwalk a long, raised stage along which models walk in fashion shows

cobbler a worker who makes or repairs shoes

corset an undergarment of fabric and stiff strips of bone or metal that ties tightly to flatten and shape the torso

cradleboard a padded board or basket, often beautifully decorated, used by early Native Americans to carry an infant

crinoline a thick, stiff undergarment worn to fill out a wide skirt

dentures artificial teeth, and the plate or frame that holds them in place

embroidery decorative, colorful stitching on a garment

face-lift a surgical operation to remove wrinkles

farthingale an undergarment made of hoops that holds a long skirt out away from the hips

liposuction a surgical operation to remove fat from a specific area of the body, such as the thighs

mercury a poisonous, silver-colored liquid metal

Mohawk a hairstyle in which all of the scalp is shaved, except for a narrow, spiky strip down the center

nose job a surgical operation to reshape the nose

pattens high-heeled shoes that slip on over one's regular shoes to keep them clean in dirty or muddy conditions

pharmacist a worker who makes or supplies healing drugs

placenta the organ that supplies blood and food to a woman's unborn baby. The placenta is delivered with the baby and is no longer needed after birth.

plastic surgery surgery to change the body or face, either to correct deformed or damaged features (called reconstructive surgery) or to make the patient look prettier (cosmetic surgery)

poacher a person who kills an animal illegally

porcelain a fragile, glassy kind of fine-quality pottery

rouge makeup that colors the cheeks red

silk a fine, smooth fabric made from threads spun by silkworms

stiletto a shoe with a very high, very skinny heel

sumptuary laws laws that limited expensive purchases and habits, often for religious reasons

tanning the treatment of animal skins to make them into soft, bendy leather.

tattoo to make a permanent pattern on the skin by rubbing or injecting color into tiny pricks or cuts

tiara a small, jeweled woman's crown, now usually worn only by queens or brides

uniform matching clothing worn to show authority or membership in a group, team, or profession. Armies, police officers, and baseball players wear uniforms.

Index

Picture credits

The publisher would like to thank the following for their kind permission to reproduce their photographs:

Position key: c=center; b=bottom; l=left; r=right; t=top

Front cover: Getty Images/Rubberball Productions (girl); Royalty-free/Corbis (glasses).

4c: R Sheridan/Ancient Art & Architecture Collection Ltd; 5l: Sunset Boulevard/Corbis; 5r: Doug Peters/allactiondigital/Empics; 6r: Brooklyn Museum of Art/Corbis; 7l: Gianni Dagli Orti/Corbis; 8l: Araldo de Luca/Corbis; 9bc: Museum of London/Heritage Image Partnership; 10r: Museum of London/Heritage Image Partnership; 10bl: Darren Sawyer; 11b: Historical Picture Archive/Corbis; 11tl: Akg-Images/Erich Lessing; 11l: Akg-Images/Erich Lessing; 11cl: Akg-Images/Erich Lessing; 12r: Araldo de Luca/Corbis; 13b: Hulton-Deutsch Collection/Corbis; 14l: Mary Evans Picture Library; 15r: 20th Century Fox/The Kobal Collection; 16br: Michael Malsan Historic Photographs/Corbis; 16l: Museum of London/Heritage Image Partnership; 17r: Adrianna Williams/ Zefa/Corbis; 19bl: Museum of London/Heritage Image Partnership; 19r: Tim Graham/Corbis; 20r: Conde Nast Archive/Corbis; 21r: Darren Sawyer; 21c: Roderick Eime-Monolith; 22l: Mary Evans Picture Library; 23r: Matthew Mendelsohn/Corbis; 23cl: Darren Sawyer; 24r: Museum of London/Heritage Image Partnership; 25tl: Hulton-Deutsch Collection/Corbis; 26l: Museum of London/Heritage Image Partnership; 27r: Akg-Images; 28bc: Science Museum/Science and Society Picture Library; 28cr: Lake County Museum/Corbis; 29r: Daniel Laine/Corbis; 30cr: Wellcome Trust; 31c: Gene Blevins/Corbis; 32cl: V&A; 32t: Museum of London/Heritage Image Partnership; 33bl: V&A; 33br: Saunders Photographic; 34bl: Wellcome Trust; 34c: Steve Jennings/Corbis; 34r: Rune Hellestad/Corbis; 35c: Science Photo Library; 36l: Photo Researchers/Corbis; 36b: Akg-Images/Erich Lessing; 37tr: Hussein Akhtar/Corbis Sygma; 37b: Akg-Images/Erich Lessing; 38r: Science Museum/Science and Society Picture Library; 39t: Science Museum/Science and Society Picture Library; 39b: Science Museum/Science and Society Picture Library; 40cr: DK Limited/Corbis; 40l: Archivo Iconografico, S.A./Corbis; 41br: Hubert Boesl/dpa/Corbis; 42r: The British Museum/Heritage Image Partnership; 43tl: Ann Ronan Picture Library/Heritage Image Partnership; 43br: Lake County Museum/Corbis; 44bl: Stephane Cardinale/People